WHEN

Does a computer sleep?

Om KIDZ
An imprint of Om Books International

Contents

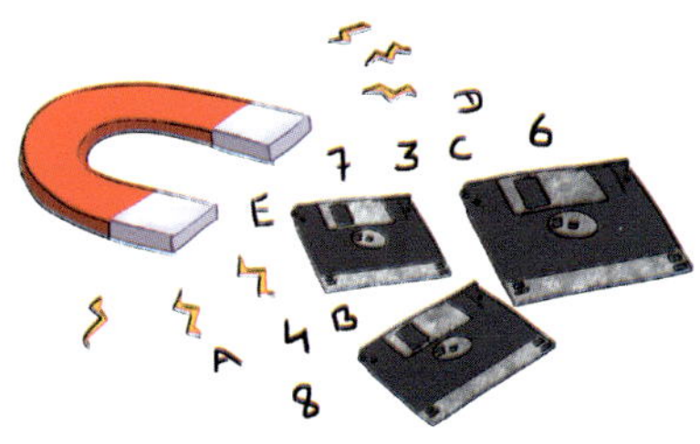

When was the word "computer" first used?

In 1613! The word "computer" was not used for a machine but to describe a human who performed calculations or computations. The definition of a computer remained the same until the end of the 19th century, when some machines were invented whose main purpose was performing calculations.

Pocket fact

The Father of Computer!
Charles Babbage was considered the Father of Computer after the invention of the Analytical Engine.

Find out

What was the Difference Engine?

When was the first mechanical computer invented?

It was proposed in 1837! The first general mechanical computer was the Analytical Engine. Its concept was proposed by Charles Babbage in 1837. The Analytical Engine contained an Arithmetic Logic Unit (ALU), basic flow control, punch cards and integrated memory. Unfortunately, because of lack of money, Charles Babbage couldn't build this computer. In 1910, Charles Babbage's youngest son, Henry Babbage completed a portion of this machine and was able to perform basic calculations.

When was the first programmable computer made?

Between 1936 and 1938! The first programmable computer was called the Z1. It was created by a German named Konrad Zuse and is considered to be the first electro-mechanical binary programmable computer, and the first really functional modern computer.

Find out

What is the full form of UNIVAC?

Pocket fact

Plankalkül!

Konrad Zuse wrote the first algorithmic programming language in 1946. It was called 'Plankalkül'.

When was the first computer company established?

In 1948! The first computer company was the Electronic Controls Company. It was founded by J. Presper Eckert and John Mauchly who also helped to create the ENIAC computer. Later, the company was renamed as Eckert-Mauchly Computer Corporation or EMCC. It also released a series of mainframe computers under the UNIVAC name.

When did computers first appear on television?

In 1952! The first computer to appear on the television was the UNIVAC 1. It was designed by the Eckert-Mauchly Computer Corporation. UNIVAC became famous in 1952 when it was used to predict who would win the presidential election between Dwight Eisenhower and Adlai Stevenson in America. As the computer predicted, Eisenhower was the winner!

Pocket fact

The BINAC Keyboard!
The BINAC Keyboard had eight keys, representing the octal numbers zero through seven. The keys when pressed produced a unique set of binary pulse codes (3 pulse combination) to give input to the computer.

Find out

Which mathematical operations could the BINAC perform?

When was the first computer designed for an aircraft company?

In 1949! The BINAC or the Binary Automatic Computer was one of the first electronic computers. It was developed for Northrop Aircraft Company and was called the BINAC or Binary Automated Computer. The computer was able to perform high-speed arithmetic operations on binary numerals.

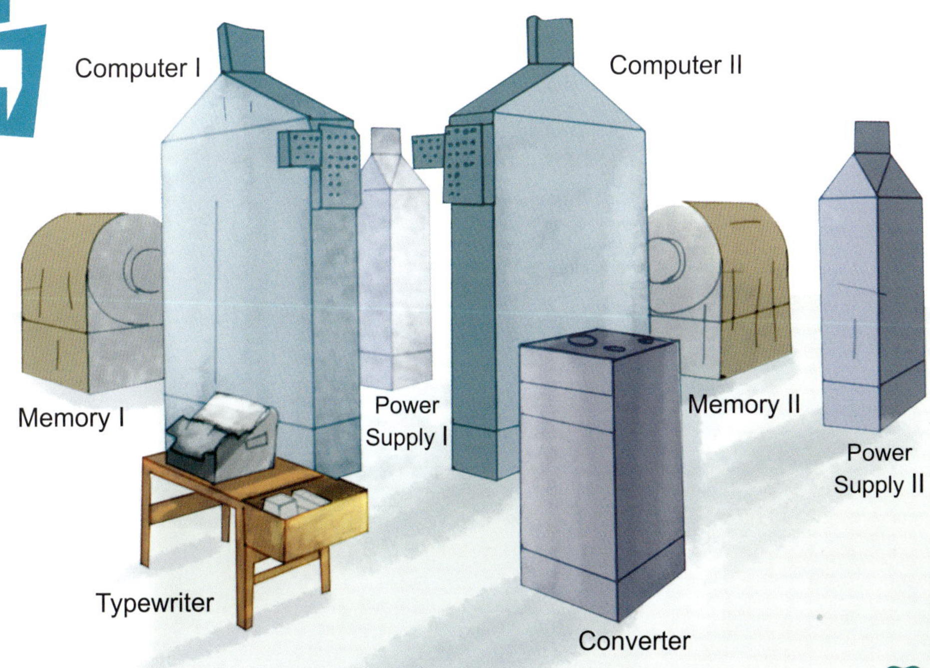

When was the first desktop computer invented?

In 1964! The first desktop computer was invented by an Italian engineer Pier Giorgio Perotto and manufactured by Olivetti. It was called the Programma 101 and was released to the public at the New York World Fair in 1964. The Programma 101 was able to perform the basic four arithmetic functions (addition, subtraction, multiplication and division), square root, absolute value, and fractional part.

Find out

When was the first personal computer invented by IBM?

Pocket fact

That's the name!

The Altair was earlier called PE-8, but Les Soloman, the writer for the Popular Electronics article wanted a catchier name. The name "Altair" was suggested by his daughter on the name of the place the Star Trek crew was travelling that week.

When was the term "personal computer" first used?

In 1975! The term "personal computer" was coined by Henry Edward Roberts when he introduced the computer Altair 8800. The computer had an Intel 8080 processor, "1024 word" memory boards with 256 bytes of memory (expandable to 64 KB). Interestingly, Altair did not have a keyboard, monitor, or printer and got its input from switches on the front of the computer. The switches represented either a 0 or a 1 and got output from flashing lights.

When was the first laptop invented?

In 1981! The first portable computer or laptop was developed by Adam Osborne. It was called the Osborne 1. It had 64 KB of memory, two 5 inch floppy drives and also included a modem.

Pocket fact

Dynabook

The first idea for a tablet computer was given by American computer scientist Alan Kay in 1972. His concept was called the Dynabook. It would be a personal computing device for children that functioned similarly to a personal computer.

Find out

When was the first tablet computer invented?

When was the palmtop computer first created?

In 1989! A palmtop computer is a personal computer that is small and light enough to be held in one hand. The first palmtop computer was called the Atari Portfolio. It was released in June 1989 by the Atari Corporation. It had a very small screen but had several built-in programs like calculator, text editor, address book, clipboard and file transfer.

When could information on a floppy disk be lost?

When it is placed near a magnet!
A floppy disk is a type of disk storage device made of thin and flexible magnetic disk inside a plastic case. It was widely used since 1970s until the early 2000s when new storage devices were invented. Since floppy disks store data in the form of magnetic fields, all its information can be lost if the disk is placed near a magnet.

Find out

What is the full form of USB?

Pocket fact

The Disgo!
The USB flash drive developed by the IBM was called the Disgo. It came in various sizes: 8 MB, 16 MB, 32 MB and 64 MB.

When were USB flash drives invented?

In 1998! The USB flash drive also commonly known as the pen drive is a data storage device. The first USB flash drive was invented by the company IBM in 1998. It was developed to replace the floppy drive in one of its product called ThinkPad.

When do bugs occur in a software?

When we make errors in designing a software! A software bug is an error, mistake, defect or fault, which may cause failure or deviation in a computer program. Most bugs are due to human errors in source code or its design, or by insufficient or erroneous logic while developing software.

Pocket fact

A buggy!
When a program contains a large number of bugs it is said to be buggy.

When does a computer become a zombie?

When it is hacked! A computer is called a zombie when it has been infected by a computer virus or compromised by a hacker. A zombie can be controlled under remote direction to perform unethical tasks, as well as infect other computers with viruses.

Find out

What signs show that your computer is infected with virus?

When was the first computer virus ever created?

In 1982! The first computer virus was written by Rich Skrenta in USA. The virus was called Elk Cloner. It spread to other computers by monitoring the floppy drive and copying itself to any floppy disk that was inserted into the computer. A computer infected with the Elk Corner would display a short poem on every 50th boot.

Find out

Why should we update antivirus softwares?

Pocket fact

A worm!

A computer worm is a destructive program that can replicate itself. It contains codes that help it enter computers or networks. Once within a computer or network, a worm can delete, modify, distribute and manipulate data.

When was the first antivirus program written?

In 1987! An antivirus is a program that protects your computer from virus. The first antivirus programs began to appear in 1987. It was an antivirus program from G Data Software for the Atari ST. Later in the same year, another antivirus program called VirusScan was introduced by John McAfee. Later, this came to be known as the McAfee antivirus program.

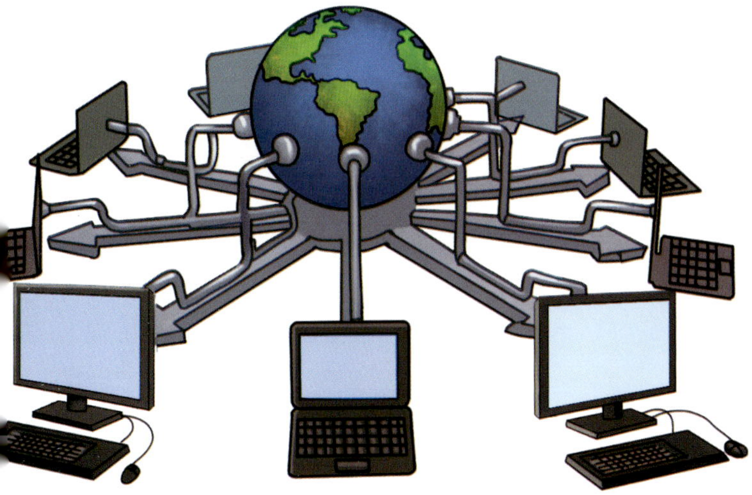

When did the Internet start?

In the late 1960s! The Internet started with the development of ARPANET that was a Wide Area Network linking many universities and research centres in the United States. It was the beginning of what we call the Internet today.

Pocket fact

Intranet!
The Intranet is a local or private network that is created using World Wide Web. It can be used only with an enterprise or organization for which it is created.

Find out

What is the difference between Internet and World Wide Web?

When was the World Wide Web introduced to people?

In 1991! The World Wide Web or WWW is a graphical interface for the Internet. It was first released on 6 August 1991 by Tim Berners Lee. The World Wide Web consists of billions of pages linked to each other. These pages contain text, graphics, multimedia files, and other interactive software that are accessed using a browser. The World Wide Web was made available to everyone on 23 August 1991.

When was the first search engine built?

In 1990! A 'web search engine' is a software system that is developed to search for information on the World Wide Web. The first search engine was called the Archie. It was created by Alan Emtage, Bill Heelan and J. Peter Deutsch, computer science students at McGill University in Montreal. Archie searched FTP sites to create an index of downloadable files.

Find out

What does CC mean in an email?

Pocket fact

Snail Mail

A mail that is sent through the post office is now-a-days called 'snail mail'. This is because it is as slow as a snail as compared to email.

When was the first email sent?

In 1971! An email or electronic mail is a method of exchanging mails between people by electronic devices. Email was invented by an American computer programmer Ray Tomlinson. He implemented the first email program on the ARPANET and sent the first email to himself as a test message.

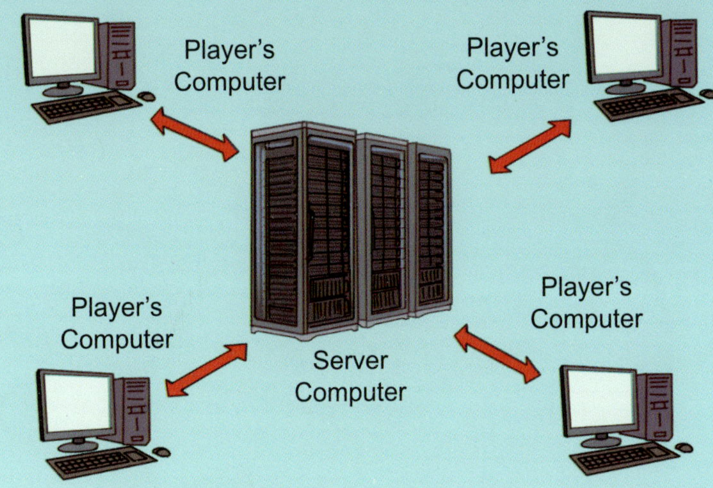

When is a computer called a server?

When it provides functionality to other programs or devices! A server is a computer program that is connected to other computers and manages network resources. It can provide different services such as control access to a network, send/receive e-mail, manage print jobs or host a website. Different computers can connect to a server through either a Local Area Network (LAN) or a Wide Area Network (WAN), such as the Internet.

Pocket fact

Mail Server!

A mail server is a remote or central computer that holds email messages for clients on a network. It is similar to a post office where mails are stored and sorted before sending them to the receiver.

Find out

How many digits are there in an IP address?

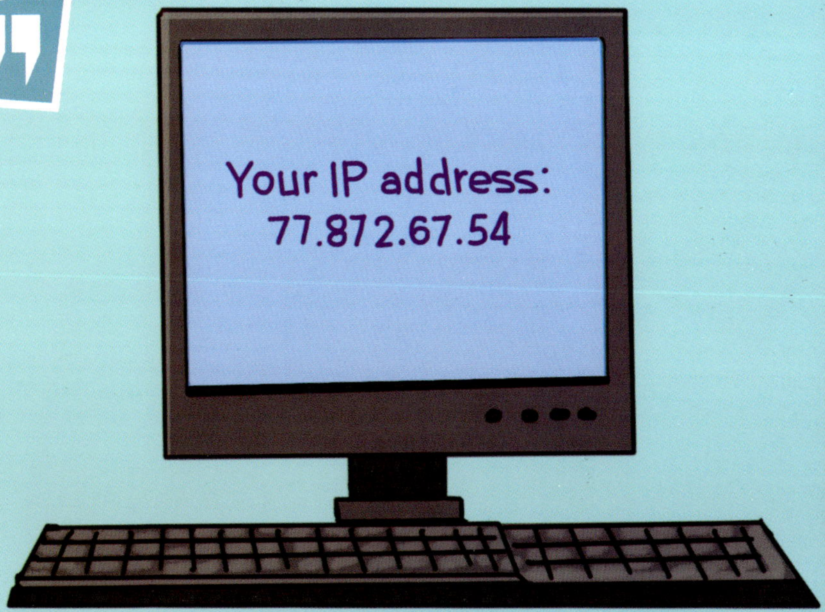

When does an address become an IP address?

When it is used to locate a computer! An IP (Internet Protocol) address is a number used to indicate the location of a computer or other device on a network. The IP address is just similar to your address, it allows data to reach the appropriate destination on a network and the Internet.

When do laptops overheat?

A laptop is said to be overheated when it generates more heat than it is designed to handle. Many times overheating is caused when a laptop's fan fails or is inadequate to cool it down. It can also occur due to poor ventilation, a bad cable, dust and dirt, an under-performing hard drive or an insufficient power supply.

Find out

What is a case fan?

Pocket fact

Revolutions per minute!

The speed of a computer or laptop fan is measured in revolutions per minute, or RPM. The higher the RPM rating, the faster the fan spins.

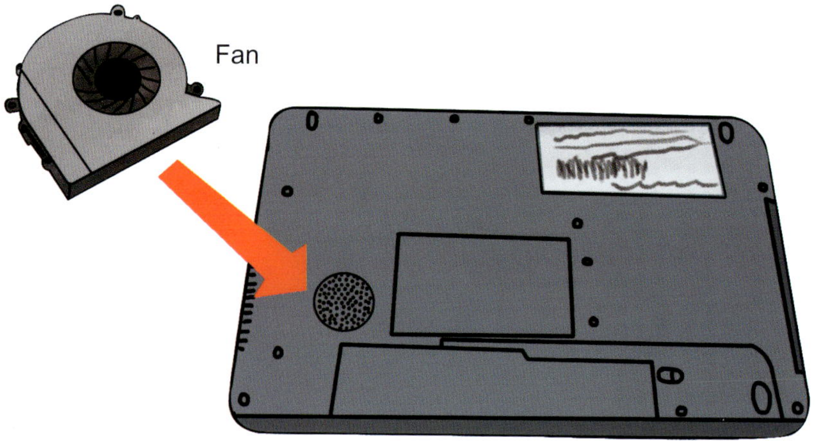

When does a laptop fan turn on?

A computer or laptop fan is a hardware device that keeps it cool by circulating air to or from the laptop or a component. Laptop fan keeps running from the moment you turn on the laptop. The fan sucks air from outside cools the device. Then, hot air is pushed out through the Fan Vent and the laptop is cooled.

When is a computer idle?

When its processor is not being used by any program! A program or task that runs on a computer system occupies a certain amount of processing time on the Central Processing Unit (CPU). When CPU has completed all its tasks and is not being used by any program, it is said to be idle.

> **Pocket fact**
>
> **The Crescent Moon!**
> You may find the crescent moon symbol on a button on your computer case or a key. This symbol is used represent night time or, in other words, going to sleep.

> **Find out**
>
> How can you wake or get a computer out of sleep mode?

When does a computer sleep?

A computer doesn't sleep by itself but you can let it enter sleep mode when it is idle for a long time! It is a period of inactivity of the computer. The Sleep mode helps the computer conserve a lot of power while it is still on.

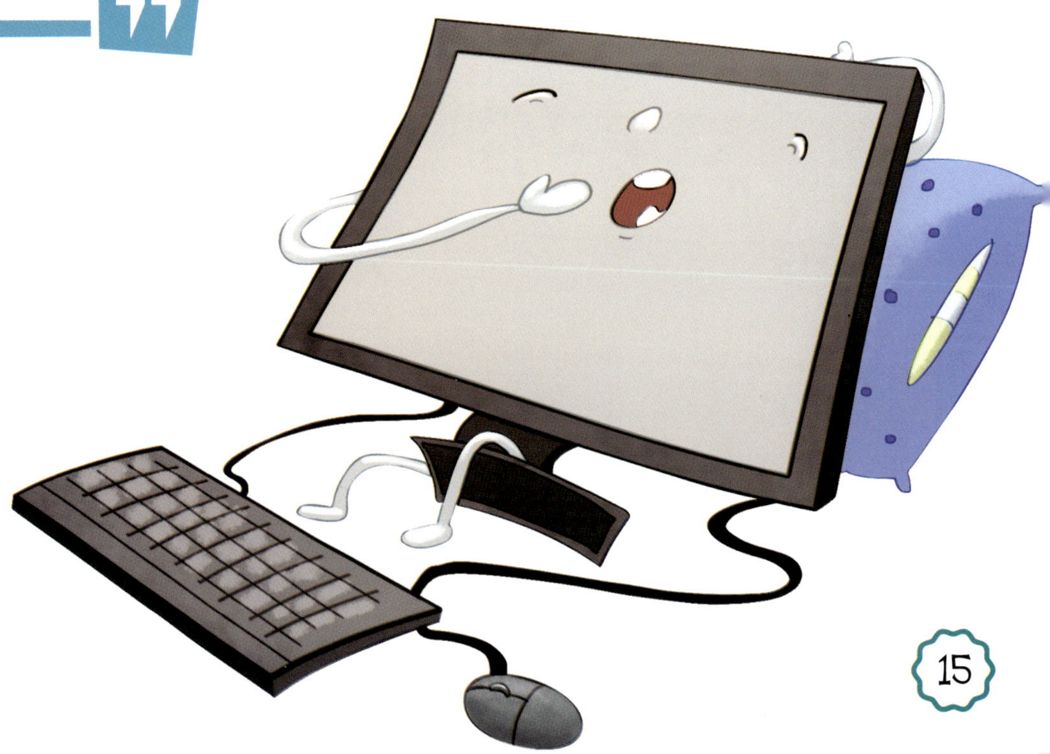

Index

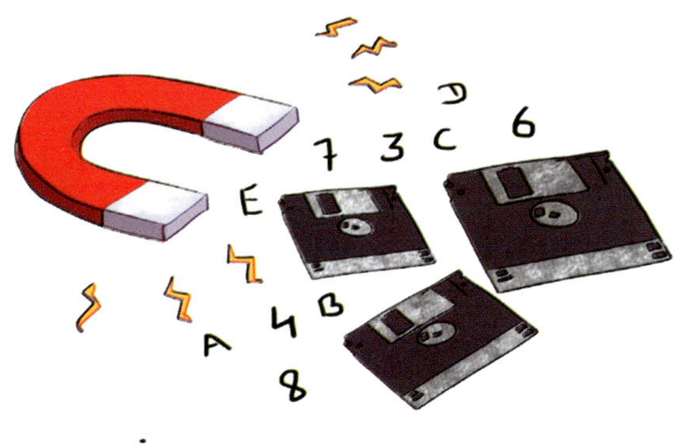